CIVIC PARTICIPATION
Working for Civil Rights

DISABILITY RIGHTS MOVEMENT

Amy Hayes

PowerKiDS
press

New York

Published in 2017 by The Rosen Publishing Group, Inc.
29 East 21st Street, New York, NY 10010

First Edition

Editor: Caitie McAneney
Book Design: Mickey Harmon

Photo Credits: Cover (image), pp. 7 (inset) Bettmann/Contributor/Bettmann/Getty Images; cover, pp. 1, 3–32 (background) Milena_Bo/Shutterstock.com; p. 5 Stephanie Keith/Stringer/Getty Images News/Getty Images; p. 7 (main), 29 wavebreakmedia/Shutterstock.com; p. 9 Heritage Images/Contributor/Hulton Archive/Getty Images; p. 10 https://commons.wikimedia.org/wiki/File:Alfred_Binet.jpg; p. 11 Stock Montage/Contributor/Archive Photos/Getty Images; p. 13 https://www.dol.gov/sites/default/files/slide7.jpg; pp. 15, 21 Wally McNamee/Corbis Historical/Getty Images; p. 17 John Preito/Contributor/Denver Post/Getty Images; p. 19 MARK SCHIEFELBEIN/Stringer/AFP/Getty Images; p. 23 Fotosearch/Stringer/Archive Photos/Getty Images; p. 25 ullstein bild/Contributor/ullstein bild/Getty Images; p. 27 https://upload.wikimedia.org/wikipedia/commons/f/f9/Atletismo_paral%C3%ADmpico_T53-54_-_front_%2828994208084%29.jpg.

Library of Congress Cataloging-in-Publication Data

Names: Hayes, Amy, author.
Title: Disability rights movement / Amy Hayes.
Description: New York : PowerKids Press, [2017] | Series: Civic
    participation: working for civil rights
Identifiers: LCCN 2016037017| ISBN 9781499426793 (pbk. book) | ISBN
    9781499426809 (6 pack) | ISBN 9781499428506 (library bound book)
Subjects: LCSH: People with disabilities–Civil rights–United
    States–Juvenile literature. | People with disabilities–Legal status,
    laws, etc.–United States–Juvenile literature. | United States. Americans
    with Disabilities Act of 1990–Juvenile literature. | Discrimination
    against people with disabilities–Law and legislation–United
    States–Juvenile literature.
Classification: LCC HV1553 .H39 2017 | DDC 323.3/20973-dc23
LC record available at https://lccn.loc.gov/2016037017

Manufactured in the United States of America

CPSIA Compliance Information: Batch #BW17PK: For Further Information contact Rosen Publishing, New York, New York at 1-800-237-9932

CONTENTS

MORE THAN A DISABILITY

People with disabilities face many challenges in their daily lives. Some have physical disabilities, while others have mental or **cognitive** disabilities. Some of these disabilities are not obvious, while others are easy to see. Whether they have a disability or not, all people define themselves by the same things: their hopes, beliefs, and thoughts. Like all people, people with disabilities wish to live full and happy lives.

People with disabilities and their allies, or supporters, work together as part of the disability rights movement. **Activists** want to make sure people with disabilities have opportunities to succeed and live as independently as possible. These activists fight **prejudice** and educate others on the needs of people with disabilities. It's been a long road, but the disability rights movement has changed many lives for the better.

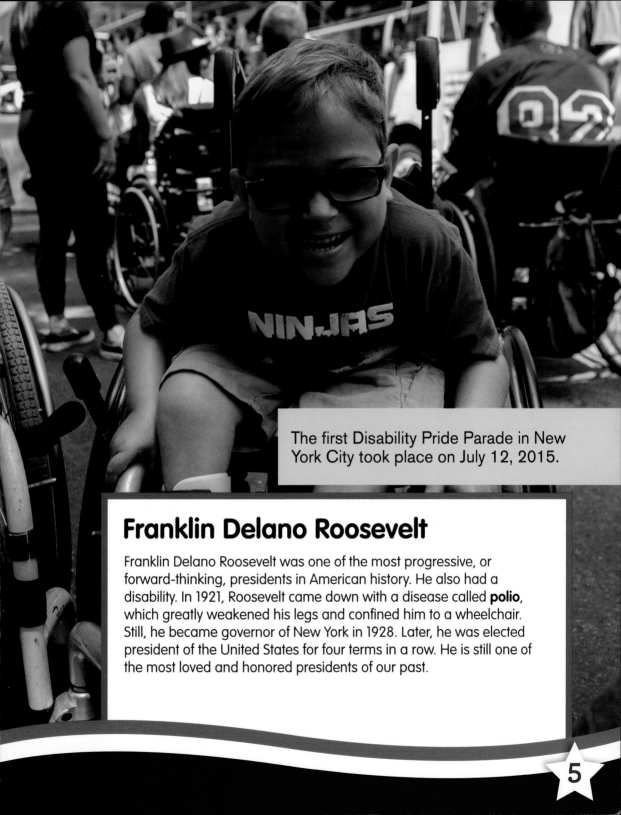

The first Disability Pride Parade in New York City took place on July 12, 2015.

Franklin Delano Roosevelt

Franklin Delano Roosevelt was one of the most progressive, or forward-thinking, presidents in American history. He also had a disability. In 1921, Roosevelt came down with a disease called **polio**, which greatly weakened his legs and confined him to a wheelchair. Still, he became governor of New York in 1928. Later, he was elected president of the United States for four terms in a row. He is still one of the most loved and honored presidents of our past.

DISCRIMINATION AGAINST PEOPLE WITH DISABILITIES

A disability is a condition, mental or physical, that prevents a person from hearing, moving, seeing, speaking, learning, or living like others. In the past, many people didn't understand the many causes of disabilities. Because of this, people with disabilities were feared or misunderstood. They faced hundreds of years of **discrimination**. Children who were born with disabilities were not always cared for, and adults with disabilities were sometimes viewed as a burden for their families.

Throughout history, this discrimination led to mistreatment and abuse. In the 1930s and 1940s, people with disabilities were some of the first to be harmed and killed when the Nazi party came to power in Germany. In the United States, people with disabilities were forced to

Some people have a disability from birth. In the past, children with disabilities lived very different lives than many children with disabilities do today. Many were separated from their families at very young ages.

HIDING PEOPLE AWAY

Even people who wanted to help make life better for people with disabilities often misunderstood their needs. They thought of disabilities as a problem that needed to be fixed. To "fix the problem," many people with disabilities were forced to live away from the rest of the community. Some were moved to poorhouses, **asylums**, and other institutions.

While these places were sometimes created to help people with disabilities, the separation usually wasn't beneficial. Because so few people visited these institutions, the places were not held to high standards. Another issue was that by keeping people with disabilities separate, communities understood them less and less. People with disabilities were ignored and forgotten, and their issues and challenges became invisible.

Bethlem Royal Hospital in London is one of the oldest hospitals for the care of mentally ill people in England. The word "bedlam" comes from the hospital's name. It is used to describe a place or situation of chaos or madness.

THE BEGINNINGS OF THE MOVEMENT

You may think movements start with one great leader, but that's not always the case. The fight for rights isn't an easy story with a start and an end. The disability rights movement, like other civil rights movements, has many players who fought different battles over hundreds of years. This is especially true of this movement because people with disabilities are incredibly diverse. That means they come from different backgrounds and deal with different challenges.

Alfred Binet

Alfred Binet was a French **psychologist** who researched intelligence. He came up with the idea of measuring a person's intelligence with a test. The score was measured on the Binet-Simon scale. The score could be used to help doctors figure out which children may have intellectual disabilities and place them in an appropriate learning environment. Binet's work helped many people understand intelligence and laid the groundwork for many child psychologists. Unfortunately, some people used Binet's test to unfairly label people and discriminate against them.

After the Civil War, wounded veterans helped raise awareness about a variety of disabilities. Even today, many veterans are active in the disability rights movement.

Wounded soldiers after the battle of Antietam

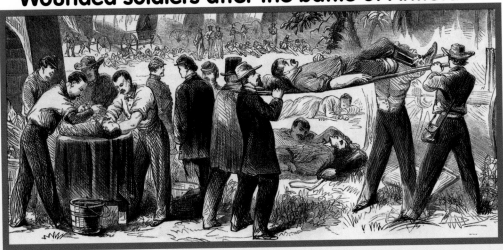

Over hundreds of years, many people made progress towards understanding and helping those with disabilities, especially as medicine improved. Advancements in **amputation** saved many lives and raised awareness of physical disabilities after the Civil War. In 1931, Clifford Beers established the International Committee of Mental Hygiene, which focused on and spread information about mental illness.

STAGING A SIT-IN

Over time, people with disabilities and their families began to speak out against injustice, and activist groups began to form. In 1921, the American Foundation for the Blind was founded. In 1935, a group of people, most of whom had **cerebral palsy** or polio, formed the League of the Physically Handicapped.

That year, the League of the Physically Handicapped sent members to stage a **sit-in** at the Home Relief Bureau in New York City. Workers at the bureau had alerted the Works Progress Administration, a program formed to provide jobs during the Great Depression, which applicants were physically handicapped. Because they were unfairly singled out, many people with disabilities were unable to get a job. The members sat for nine days. The press told their story to the world and they gathered support. Eventually, they won thousands of jobs for people with disabilities.

HIRE THE HANDICAPPED *through*
State Employment Service Local Offices

This poster came out in 1951, 16 years after the League of the Physically Handicapped won its first battle.

Civil Disobedience

A sit-in is an act of civil disobedience. Civil disobedience is when people refuse to obey a law to protest something they feel is unfair. The point of civil disobedience is to bring attention to issues you think aren't right and to change things for the better. Many civil rights activists—including Mohandas Gandhi, Martin Luther King Jr., and students protesting the Vietnam War—employed civil disobedience.

WORKING TOWARD EQUALITY

Much of the legal action towards progress in the disability rights movement began in the late 1900s. The American civil rights movement, which fought for African American rights, sparked social change for many other groups. This movement not only inspired activists fighting for people with disabilities but also showed ways for lawmakers to improve the quality of life for certain groups.

In 1973, the Rehabilitation Act was passed. Section 504, part of this act, was based on previous laws that banned discrimination based on race, sex, or background by programs and businesses that receive federal funding. Section 504 showed that lawmakers recognized that the problems of people with disabilities were caused in part by prejudice and discrimination and that new laws were needed.

During the 1970s, many different groups protested for equal rights. Members of the disability rights movement made great progress because of their activism.

COMING TOGETHER

The Rehabilitation Act of 1973 was a very important piece of legislation for the disability rights movement. Section 504 stated that no federally funded program could discriminate against people with disabilities. It declared that these programs must meet the reasonable needs of people with disabilities, which was especially important for students with disabilities. Under this law, public schools had to meet the educational needs of all students with disabilities.

Before this legislation, smaller **advocacy** groups existed for certain disabilities, but they were separate from one another. When Section 504 was created, people with different types of disabilities—physical and mental, visible or invisible—had the same protection under the law. Since this law covered all people with disabilities, it made those people and their allies a stronger and more united front.

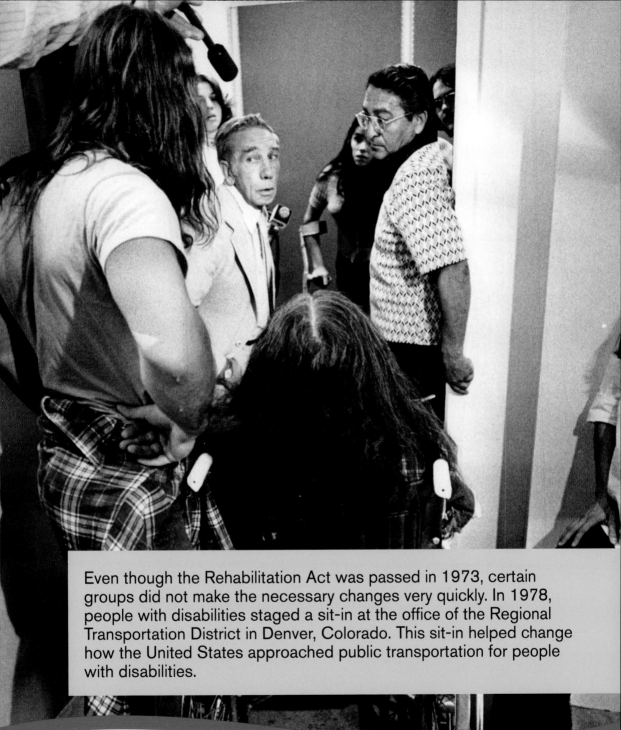

Even though the Rehabilitation Act was passed in 1973, certain groups did not make the necessary changes very quickly. In 1978, people with disabilities staged a sit-in at the office of the Regional Transportation District in Denver, Colorado. This sit-in helped change how the United States approached public transportation for people with disabilities.

A CONSTANT LEADER

Leaders in the disability rights movement are an impressive force against the silencing and separation of people with disabilities. One important leader is Judith Heumann. As a child, Heumann came down with polio. She has used a wheelchair for most of her life. When she was young, her parents had to fight for her right to attend school with other students. In college, she organized other people with disabilities to fight to make classes more accessible. She wanted to become a teacher, but she had to fight for that right as well.

From 1993 to 2001, Heumann served as the assistant secretary for the Office of Special Education and Rehabilitative Services in the U.S. Department of Education. In 2010, Heumann was appointed a special advisor for international disability rights to the U.S. Department of State.

Judith Heumann has worked for the rights of people with disabilities for most of her life. Now, she helps people with disabilities around the world.

A GREAT IDEA

One of the major challenges for children with disabilities was access to education. They were often kept from getting the same education as other students. This kept people with disabilities separate, and separate is never equal.

When the Education for All Handicapped Children Act was passed in 1975, all children finally had a right to equal education. Many students with disabilities were **integrated** into classrooms. They were now able to learn alongside children without disabilities. Not only did students with disabilities get a better education, but other students had a chance to learn about, accept, and include people who are different from them.

In 1990, this legislation was renamed the Individuals with Disabilities Education Act (IDEA). It gave parents more rights when deciding what type of education their children should receive. It is one of the greatest victories for disability rights so far.

In 1997, President Bill Clinton signed amendments to IDEA to make sure that all children in America receive equal opportunities for their education.

AMERICANS WITH DISABILITIES ACT

After decades of organizing and working hard to be heard, Americans with disabilities celebrated a huge victory in 1990 when the Americans with Disabilities Act (ADA) became law. The ADA is a federal law that ensures businesses and agencies provide **accommodations** so people with disabilities have equal opportunities for jobs and equal access to public spaces and services.

The law states that businesses have to accommodate people's different abilities with changes such as special work equipment and flexible hours. The law ensures that people who use wheelchairs have access to public transportation across the country. Also, people with mental illness may have a chance to work changeable hours, which may help them balance their illness and their job. These are just some of the accommodations possible for people with disabilities.

President George H. W. Bush, at right, signed the ADA into law. This act provides service and support for people with disabilities throughout the nation.

A SHELTERED PLACE

Today, many people with disabilities apply for jobs and find work on their own. However, for people with severe disabilities, this is not always possible. Sometimes people with severe cognitive disabilities need close direction, and they need a job that fits their personal strengths. Many of these people work at sheltered workshops.

However, many sheltered workshops are closing. Some people think this is a good thing because the workshops prevent people with disabilities from working with other people in the community. Most sheltered workshops don't pay very much.

Other people worry that people with severe disabilities will be treated badly or fired in a regular workplace. To them, these workshops are a safe space where people can feel productive, make friends, and continue to work throughout adulthood.

People who work in sheltered workshops have different opinions about them. Some like coming to a safe space every day, but some want to have a more traditional job.

What's a Sheltered Workshop?

A sheltered workshop is a place where people with disabilities work at tasks that fit their level of skill in a controlled setting. They are paid, but the amount is much below the minimum wage. However, the close management, accommodating workspace, and lack of stress can give people a safe place to be productive. Many workshops provide social events and settings so people with disabilities can interact with their coworkers and make friends.

MOVING FORWARD

Fighting prejudice isn't easy, and educating others about disability issues is a huge undertaking. That's partly because there are so many different types of disabilities.

However, there has been much progress in the fight for the rights of people with disabilities. The United States has come very far in terms of legislation, accommodations, and views about people with disabilities, but we still have more work to do.

People with disabilities are an important part of society. Many live productive and independent lives. They want to be accepted for their abilities, not just seen for their disabilities. If the disability rights movement has taught us anything, it is that we can become a stronger community together.

The Special Olympics and Paralympics

There are two main international sporting events for people with disabilities. The Paralympic Games were founded in Italy in 1960 for athletes with physical disabilities. The first Special Olympics were held in 1968. The Special Olympics are for people with cognitive disabilities. Both of these events celebrate the skills of people with disabilities, and remind others that people with disabilities can compete at a high level.

The Paralympics and Special Olympics show us that people with disabilities have exceptional talents.

ACTIVATE YOUR INNER ACTIVIST

Have you thought about what you can do to help the disability rights movement? It's a **complicated** issue, but that doesn't mean that helping has to be. Ask your local children's hospital if there are any fund raisers coming up. There are many different ways to raise money for a cause, including running, walking, or biking as part of a fund-raising event. These fund raisers increase awareness of different disabilities and help raise money for programs and research.

One in five people in the United States has a disability. You probably know at least one person. If you know someone with a disability, ask them how you can help. Listen closely. If you have a disability, get involved in your community and speak out against discrimination. There are many great ways to advocate for other people with disabilities, and yourself too!

The fight for equal rights for people with disabilities continues today.

TIMELINE OF THE DISABILITY RIGHTS MOVEMENT

1865
The Civil War ends. Because of advancements in military medicine, many men survive having limbs amputated. This raises society's awareness of people with physical disabilities.

1918
World War I ends. Many men come home shell-shocked, which is a mental disorder that is now called post-traumatic stress disorder, or PTSD. This raises society's awareness of people with mental illness.

1933
Franklin D. Roosevelt, who developed polio in 1921, becomes president. He serves until 1945.

1935
The League of the Physically Handicapped holds a sit-in at the Home Relief Bureau in New York City.

1973
Section 504 of the Rehabilitation Act is passed. Section 504 bans discrimination based on disability.

1975
The Education for All Handicapped Children Act is passed.

1977
The San Francisco sit-in in support of Section 504 brings people with all different types of disabilities together to protest for nearly a month.

1990
The Americans with Disabilities Act (ADA) is passed. This groundbreaking law ensures people with disabilities have access to employment services and public places, and protects against discrimination.

GLOSSARY

accommodation: Something to satisfy a need.

activist: Someone who acts strongly in support of or against an issue.

advocacy: The action of supporting or speaking in favor of something.

amputation: A surgery to remove a person's limb.

asylum: In the past, a hospital where people who were mentally ill were cared for, especially for long periods of time.

cerebral palsy: A disorder in which a person has problems moving and speaking.

cognitive: Relating to intellectual activity, or the ability to think in a logical way.

complicated: Having many parts; difficult to explain or understand.

discrimination: Treating people unequally because of their race, beliefs, background, or lifestyle.

integrate: To make a person or group part of a larger group.

polio: A disease that sometimes damages the spinal cord, making movement difficult.

prejudice: An unfair feeling of dislike for a person or group because of race, religion, sex, lifestyle, or disability.

psychologist: Someone who studies the science of the mind and behavior.

sit-in: A protest in which people sit or stay in a place and refuse to leave.

INDEX

WEBSITES

Due to the changing nature of Internet links, PowerKids Press has developed an online list of websites related to the subject of this book. This site is updated regularly. Please use this link to access the list: www.powerkidslinks.com/civic/disa